The Magical Power
of My Praying Parents

Heavenly Realm Publishing
Houston, TX

Minnett Pommells

Copyright © 2023 – The Magical Power of My Praying Parents, Minnett Pommells, all rights reserved.

All rights reserved. This book is protected by the copyright laws of the United States of America. This book may not be copied or reprinted for commercial gain or profit.

Published by: Heavenly Realm Publishing, www.heavenlyrealmpublishing.com, 1-866-216-0696

ISBN 13 – 9781944383-36-7 (soft cover)
ISBN 13 – 9781944383-37-4 (hard cover)

1. Biography: Autobiography/Personal Memoirs – United States. 2. Biography: Autobiography/Religious – United States. 3. Biography: Autobiography/General – United States.

This book is available at: Amazon, Barnes & Noble, Books-A-Million, Borders, and stores near you.

This book is printed on acid free paper.

This book is printed in the USA.

The Magical Power
of My Praying Parents

My Praying Father

My Praying Mother

Table of Contents

Introduction 7

Chapter One:

    Holland Bamboo, In St. Elizabeth 11

    The Community Midlife 14

    The Miracle Breadfruit 18

    The Donkey Charlie 20

    The Faithful Dog 21

    Faith and Prayer 28

    God's Favor 30

Chapter Two:

    My Prayer Answered and My Change Came 33

Introduction

Jamaica is an island placed in the Caribbean Sea. It has beautiful beaches mysterious mountains, vast numbers of rivers, breath taking beauty and lush vegetation.

Growing up on the island, everything seems magical. The beauty of the plants and trees as they change in their seasons. The blooming of different plants and fruit trees each producing times. There is always something to eat.

The constant changes — babies being born, children growing up, older children leaving home to pursue their career, days turn to weeks, weeks turn to months and months turn into years.

But most of all to observe the blessings of God's creation and the Magical answers to my parent's prayers.

Chapter One

I was born on the island of Jamaica Parish of Manchester in the nineteen fifties. Jamaica at that time was a very religious island. There were many different religious denominations on the island.

In those days, prayer was the only comfort to many people. My parents were among those who's prayer and faith in God brought them through many difficult times.

In the year of 2020 with the Covid-19 pandemic, we needed lots of prayer and faith in God to deliver us from this crisis. I know God hears the prayer of his children and He still answers prayer.

I was blessed to be the tenth and last child born to my parents, Mr. and Mrs. Hyman and Dinata Pommells. We were six girls and four boys. We grew up in Manchester which is in the middle of the island. Our parents also grew up here. Manchester is known for its beautiful women and fruitfulness. Our parents were farmers and mother were also a seamstress and self-taught midwife.

They were of the Christian faith—going to church, praying and going to school was the foundation of our upbringing. Every Sunday morning at 6:00am, mother would ring her little prayer bell and say loudly, "it's prayer time!" It didn't matter if you were a visitor or how old you were, you were expected to be present for prayer around that wooden table. That was not the only the time we prayed, that was the time we prayed as a family, giving thanks for the end of one week and the beginning of another. This was also in preparation for Sunday church.

How beautiful is the Creators great works. The leaves of the tall coconut and palm trees wave in the wind. Sugar cane fields waving their blossom and leaves in the wind. Golden hairs of corn shining in the sun. The blue oceans white foam outlines the beauty of the island. The lush green foliage of the mountain's peaks reaching toward the blue skies, breathtaking beauty. Duns River falls, one of many beautiful waterfalls on the island. Fern Gully with its think foliage of fern forming a canopy along the road making it very cool and quiet. These are on the Northern side of the island. On the Southern side of the island, you will find Holland Bamboo. This is miles of beautiful bamboo trees forming a curtain and canopy over the roadway. It's a great place to relax for some inner peace and thoughts. There are many more beautiful breathtaking sceneries that makes you think God must be very proud He created this beautiful little island.

Holland Bamboo, In St. Elizabeth

My father who was very handsome and light-skinned was raised by his mother who was African Indian and Aunts who were of French descents. Unfortunately, they didn't see the need for him to get an education. Therefore, my father could not read or write. When I started school at six years old, I became his teacher. He was a good student. Soon he was able to read and write his name. My father was quite a man, and very proud of his family. He was up at four thirty every morning praying for his family, his animals and his farm. His main prayer to God was asking Him not to take him from this world until his last child passed the worst.

God did answer his prayer.

My father was a silent praying man. He was a quiet man until someone messed with his children or his animals. He taught me to appreciate and observe the night skies. Several nights I would sit with my father outside. We would look at the stars as he could tell when it was going to rain and when it was going to be a sunny day. He would look up at the sky and talk to God as if he was talking to a friend, telling him about his family, "Please help my children to have a better life, please provide for all their needs, guide and protect those living in the city (Kingston), let them live their lives serving You." That was his way of praying at times.

My father's rule was simple, he said, "follow the golden rule, go to school, do not beg, do not borrow, if you do not have it do without it, respect your elders and BLOODLY HELL DO NOT STEAL."

Mother was a magical woman. Every morning, you could hear her praying for her children, calling out their names in order of birth, from the first to the last child. "Father, please bless my children and protect them. Please keep them safe. Raise them up to be of service to You." This was always a part of her prayer. Mother, I can say, had a very strong faith in God, which I realized at an early age. Sometimes we would not have food in the house, we would hear my mom talking to God, standing in the doorway of the kitchen. I was always looking to see who was with her. Sometimes I would ask, "Momma, who are you talking to?" Her reply was, "My Father in Heaven. I am asking Him to provide for our dinner tonight because I don't have anything to cook. Go put a pot of water on and let's go check the bean tree and the garden to see what we can find." Each time this is what would happen if we found something in the garden to cook and had no meat, someone would show up with money owing my parents. My mother would say, "See my dear, God provides for them so they can pay their debt. If we had meat and no food after she prays, some food would come.

Then she would say, "My dear, God will always provide. As long as you ask Him and believe." So, from a young age, I have experienced the power of prayer. When hard times would fall, there was always a special place my mother would stand and talk with God that was between the kitchen in the house and facing towards the Mile Gully Mountain. Her favorite quote was, "I will lift my eyes unto the hills from whence cometh my help, my help cometh from God who makes Heaven and earth." As a child, I always wondered who lived in the Mile Gully Mountain and heard my momma praying and always sent help. It never failed; somebody was always coming with something. I know my mother had a strong connection with God, so I stayed close to her.

Mother was very active in her church. I remember going with her when it was our turn to clean the church. It was my pride and joy to polish and shine the benches and the floor with the coconut brush and beeswax. We would play music on the floor with the brush.

Mother was also a strong leader in the church and community. When it's the women's day at church, my mother's topic was mostly based on faith, love peace and prayer. She was the leader of the prayer group. My mother prayed for everyone anytime and anywhere. Momma would pray about anything that was given to her. If you gave her a glass of water, she would pray over it. Her reason was, "My dear, the hands offering may not be clean, but the heart is clean. The hands be clean, but the heart not clean. Only God knows, you don't. So always bless what's offered to you."

I grew up knowing and seeing the effects and power of prayer. Therefore, I learned to pray with faith at an early age. Prayer was my mother's weapon against any and everything.

Anyone who knows my mother will tell you she is a woman of faith and prayer.

When I listened to my mother pray, I got the feeling of talking to a bosom friend. She told of her children by name. She told of their achievements and their weaknesses. She would ask God to give them knowledge and for them to know Him to pray and live for Him. I would imagine God's big ear listening over the house to whenever she prayed. I can say her prayers were always answered from what I have seen and the testimony of the people she prayed for. Sometimes we would hear her say, "thank you Father, thank You my God. You are always providing for us." I would ask, "Momma what did you get?" She would say, "Not yet my dear, but soon you will see." Sometimes a day a two may pass and sure enough, something will always show up that's greatly needed.

The Community Midlife

Mother was known in our community and surrounding communities for her answered prayers. People would come to church with testimonies of the result of mother's prayers. Mother would be the first to know of any pregnancies in the communities. The women would schedule their deliveries with her early, even though she had no formal medical training. She would always pray for guidance to bring this child into the world, to be of service to God. She has never lost a baby or a mother. Mother delivered her last baby in her later sixties. It was amazing how many young men and women mother delivered in this world. She was not afraid to encourage and pray for anyone, young or old, of any nationality. Mother was loved and known for her kindness and prayers.

On Vacation With Mother

Farming was our main source of income in Jamaica. Most of our church members were farmers. Every Monday when it's the season for planting, they would get together and work on each other's farm. I always loved going to the farm if it was not a school day. The women would do the cooking and also help with planting crops. While they worked, they would pray and sing as they used their working tools as musical instruments. There were several farmers in the area. In the distance you could hear the melodies of other farmers echo, joining in singing and praying.

The birds and other creatures would join in with their chirping or whatever sound they made. It seems they too were giving thanks and praise. Mother was greatly involved in planting crops. On several occasions, mother would plant yellow yam. While she planted, she would pray asking God to bless the crops so she could meet the needs of her family. When it was time to reap this yam mother planted, men took turns digging what looked like a giant hand stuck in the ground. It was a task getting it whole, most times they would cut the fingers off. I remembered mother saying, "God does answer prayer."

Those produce would be sold to the agricultural market for export. As mentioned, everything has its season. During the summertime, school would be out, and it would be reaping time for the corn fields. This period was a fun time for both adults and for children. Church members took turns reaping corn from each other's farm. To get corn ready for the market it has to be removed from the cob. Corn shelling was usually done on a Friday night. Members of the church would gather for what was called a shelling match. This would be done with singing and praying all night until all corn is collected.

A meal of bammy, fried fish, fried dumpling, potato pudding, coffee, hot chocolate or tea would be served. Sometimes other people from the community would join in as there was always plenty of food.

We call it Mile Gully Mountain. This is during the times when mother prayed.

The Magical Power of My Praying Parents

Mile Gully Mountain

"I will lift up mine eyes unto the hills, from whence cometh my help, my help cometh from the Lord, which made Heaven and earth."

Psalm 121

Every Wednesday, there were praying and fasting at church. You would not have breakfast or lunch. Sometimes prayer continued from the early morning until 3:00pm in the afternoon. People would bring their prayer requests or sick family members for prayer.

Praying and fasting were strongly encouraged as to build strong faith in God. People would testify of the effect or result of prayer and how they have been healed from sickness, obtained jobs, children's grades improved, or they were accepted into high school or college. There were always positive results reported in relation to praying and fasting. Many times, the prayer group would be called for prayer at somebody's house. At times they would be there all day. There was always effective change. In any situation, prayer was the first consultation, medicine or weapon to be used. Amazingly there would always be a positive result.

The Miracle Breadfruit

Breadfruit is a staple food in Jamaica. It grows on a very large tree. Its name suggest that it can be used as bread, and when ripe, it is used as a fruit for making smoothies. Breadfruit in its young stage can also be used as a vegetable. It is very good in beef soup. You can bake, boil, and roast breadfruit. It can be eaten with any meat. It is used as a substitute for rice, potatoes, or yams. Breadfruit also has its bearing season.

I was about twelve years old and for whatever reason, I did not go to school that day. Mother was in the house reading her Bible. I was outside doing chores. The street from the main road down to our village ends on the hill at our home. I heard a lady's voice calling my mother's name. Mother heard it as well and said, "I don't know that voice." And I said, "I don't either." The calling got closer to the house. Finally, mother answered. I had checked on this lady, and yes, she was a stranger. Mother invited her up, entry point between the house and the kitchen. They greeted each other and the lady acknowledged me also. She said, "Ma' me I know we don't know each other, but I was sent by a lady at Buck Up (that's an adjoining district about a mile from our home). I have nothing to feed my children so the lady said I should ask for directions to your home. You might be able to help me, even to give me a Breadfruit that would be of great help."

I remember hearing my mother say, "My dear lady, I am sorry, but Breadfruit season is long gone." Mother invited the lady in the house. They sat and talked for a while. During this time, mother was telling the lady about God, His mercies, and His promises. She prayed with the lady. Mother will not let this lady go home empty handed. On that day we had very little of anything. Mother called me and told me to wrap half of the small amount of sugar and bring it to her. This she gave it to the lady. As the lady was about to leave, mother stopped and looked at the Breadfruit tree, and again repeated, "I am so sorry you walked this far, and I have nothing to give you." But the lady thanked her for her prayer, and the very small amount of sugar. As the lady proceeded to walk away, I heard mother say, "Wait my dear, wait!" Then she called me and said, "Your eyes are younger than mine. I want you to look up there." She pointed high up in the Breadfruit tree. "Tell me, is that a Breadfruit?" She asked.

I was excited to see a huge Breadfruit looking at us as it sat high up in the tree. I said, Momma, it's a big Breadfruit."

Mother said to the lady, "My sister, you came for Breadfruit and there it is. But how are you going to get it?" I was a skinny girl and always climbing trees, so I offered to go pick it for them. I climbed up the ladder, scampered up the tree, using the hook stick and picked that huge Breadfruit for the lady. When my mother placed it in her hands, she told her, "God will always provide for His children as long as you believe Him and pray." I remember the smile on that lady's face. She was walking with a spring in her step, clutching that big Breadfruit close to her chest. Mother said to me, "Well my dear, you have witnessed a miracle today. Always trust God and you will be alright."

Breadfruit

The Donkey Charlie

Our farm was about three miles from home at Mizpah. You could get there by walking or riding a donkey. My father's donkey was named "Charlie." This animal was very intelligent and unique. He was our transportation for any occasion. He understood directions and instructions. On days when mother would go alone to the farm at Mizpah, she left at about 8:00am.

Mother would get the donkey ready, then she prays after she told the donkey, "okay boy, we're going to Mizpah today, let's go." The donkey's behavior with mother was always gentle and understanding.

Leaving from our house on the hill, she passed five homes before getting to the main road. While she stopped to talk with the neighbors, the donkey continued his journey. People in the district and adjoining district to Mizpah knew the donkey and to whom it belonged to. They also knew not to try getting into his hamper (basket). The donkey on reaching the major highway crossing to get to the farm will not cross until mother got there. On several occasions, the donkey waited for a good while because mother stopped to talk and pray with people along the way.

My father and the donkey had a different relationship. They would always argue and fight. My father had a full conversation with the donkey, and he seemed to understand. Father would talk to God while getting the donkey ready for their journey. Charlie knew the difference between prayer and a conversation with him and not to disturb father when he was praying. Father always shared his food and drinks with the donkey. The donkey drank coffee from a cup and beer from the bottle, but he never got drunk. The donkey knew his way home from wherever they went.

The Faithful Dog

Our faithful dog's name was Keneis. Keneis was a common brown and white dog. He knew my father's work schedule. He would wait every morning outside the steps of my parent's room for my father. He goes with him to milk the cows and ties the goats for feeding.

My father worked for the Bauxite Company preparing land for mining. Every morning and evening, the Bauxtie Company would sound an alarm at 8:00am to start working, and at 4:30pm, to stop working so that all employees knew to leave by 5:00pm when the second alarm went off.

My father has a small farm called, "Happy Hut," not far from the house. You could see it from our house on the hill. Every evening, the dog would leave to meet my father at "Happy Hut." One evening Keneis came home in a hurry without my father. Mother was cooking in the kitchen, and the dog came in barking at her, running back and forth in the direction going towards the bottom of the property where my father would stop in the evenings.

My mother and I had decided to follow the dog. Keneis took us where my father was sitting; bleeding from a wound to his arm he sustained while he was cutting something and slipped. My mother bandaged the wound with the apron she was wearing and prayed while doing so. We got father up the hill to the house where she cleaned and dressed the wound. The dog didn't leave my father's side.

One day we saw the dog not looking well and did not go to meet my father. My father came home to find the dog sick. Surely he called mother, and she came and the only thing she could do was pray for the dog. That was a very sad day as we sat there and prayed for the dog. Mother usually said, "We've done all we can, let him rest." In a few days the dog was well and doing his friendly duties.

My first financial advisors were my parents. They taught me the value of a penny, a shilling and a pound. These were the British currency used in Jamaica while under the British rule. At the age of eleven years old, I would go with my parents to the market and sell produce from the farm. They took pride in the presentation of produce for sale.

I did not like dirt underneath my nails. I was also afraid of worms or any crawling insects. My produce for sale was dried corn and peas. Those were sold by quart, pint and half pint. Sales were never the exact measurement, number or weight. My parents taught me to always add some blessing. Meaning, add one or two extra fruit and a few ounces to your weight and extra to your measurement. In other words, make your dozen be thirteen, and in all your doings be honest.

I always got my tips which I learned to save. At times I would use some of my money for lunch but had enough to get what I needed. When I got older and started earning a salary, I saw the need for investing, how to budget and save. I have invested in children, nieces and nephews. My parents always said to remember where you are from and help those in need. My parent's prayers have still been answered. I think there is a big smile on my father's face to see the accomplishments of his children, knowing he was denied the opportunity of education.

God continues to answer my parent's prayers (Please keep my children safe). While living in Jamaica, I was working at the City Hospital in Kingston. One evening at the end of my shift, I was singing and walking down Orange Street, going toward the town to catch my bus to get home. Usually this is a very busy street from above the hospital down to the Ocean front. As I was walking about the second block from the hospital, I heard a voice on my left coming from over a fence yell, "its okay, it's my little nurse. Nurse hurry and get to town!" I looked to where the voice was coming from but saw no one. Only then I realized the street was empty and I was the only person on the street in the middle of a turf war. I could see the ocean clearly from where I was standing no one in sight. That was my sprinting signal, and the fastest sprinter would not have passed me getting in the town.

A few years after my father passed away, I migrated to New York. After getting my orientation to the bus and subway system, I was ready for New York. One day I got a sitting assignment at a hospital on First Avenue in Manhattan. I had to take the subway and walk a few blocks to the hospital. At the end of my shift about 9:00pm, I was singing and walking toward the subway station, again about the second block from the hospital to my left I heard this voice say, "nurse hurry and get to the subway." I went into sprint mode to the subway as instructed with no questions asked. On another occasion I got an assignment in the Bronx travelling via the subway. I took the subway, got off at the right station in Harlem but got out on the wrong side. I started singing and walking until I met the wall separating Bronx from Harlem. I made a right turn only then I saw some one and ask for direction to the address I was going to. The person was nice and gave me directions. After walking a few blocks and getting on this Bronx side, I found the address.

When I got to the lady's house and explained to her why I was late. The lady put her hands on her head and said, "Oh my God did you see anyone on the street in Harlem?"

I answered, "no mam.'"

She said, "my dear, God was with you." I thought for a second then asked her "why she thought that?"

Her reply was, "this is one of the most dangerous places in the city." Its then I realized that I saw no one until I made that right turn at the wall.

Yea, though I walk through the valley of the shadow of death, I will fear no evil, for thou art with me, thy rod and thy staff they comfort me (Psalm 23:4).

I remember my father's prayer was asking God not to take him from this world until his last child passed the worst. My father left this world in December 1981. Here's the accomplishment of the children whose father was denied an education but who's prayer God did answer.

Children in order to birth:
1. Mechanical Engineer
2. Seamstress/ CNA
3. Shoe Manufacturer
4. Carpenter/ Shoe Manufacturer
5. Seamstress/ CNA
6. License Practical Nurse
7. Secretary/ Insurance Agent
8. Interior Decorator/ Shoe Manufacturer
9. Member of the women cricket club/ CNA
10. Registered Nurse/ Author. I am the last child when my father died. I was in the second year of my nursing career.

Now, did God answer his prayer?

Father's prayer continues to be answered.

The blessings of his grandchildren as follows and I'm aware of:

1. Architect
2. Accountant
3. Business Owners
4. Computer Engineer/ Tech.
5. Court Clerk
6. Doctor
7. Electrical Engineer
8. Financial Crime Advisor

9. HR Manager/ Supervisor
10. Mechanical Engineer
11. Nurse, Certified Nursing Assistant
12. Navy Officer, Police
13. Preacher/ Bishop
14. Respiratory Therapist
15. Structural Engineer and many more. I'm sure, the blessing and answered prayer continues.

Father and Sisters in Heaven

Each day as I'm awaken to the beauty of God's creation, I give Him thanks. Each time I revisit my life's journey, I am grateful for God's blessing, grace and His great mercy. Prayer has always been my source of strength all my life. In the medical field, you have to pray so your work will not be in vain. Many times, my assignment seems so impossible; the only way to start, was to pray. At times I remembered my parents praying and mother calling my name as she would when praying. Sometimes I would pray for, and with my patients, some at their request and others it was their added medication (Prayer). At times at work, I just had to pray for help whether it was a strong arm, additional staff or spiritual help. But I know when I pray things change.

During the Covid-19 Pandemic, I realized the need and power of prayer. It was a very dark time for the world, but people found courage to pray for each other. Praying in different languages all over the world for people you know and those you do not know. My prayers are with the medical staff. I know firsthand what they were facing. It was a good feeling when people were requesting prayer for medical personal. They needed spiritual guidance and help during this pandemic. Caring for the sick and the dying, you have to give your all. Prayer is what kept me going these forty years.

There was a day I had to work a double shift due to shortage of staff. I returned to work eight hours later the following day for my assigned shift. I opened the door at the staff entrance to the hospital and heard a voice saying, "I can do all things through Christ Who strengthens me." I looked around to see who was talking to me and saw no one. I opened the door and with new strength, I continued to my assigned unit.

Upon returning home that night, mother said to me, "it's only the mercy of God that's keeping you alive for His service." I did not eat the lunch she made for me because I was rushing not wanting to be late. I reflect on my parent's prayers for their children still being effective on our lives. God is still answering our parent's prayers. He did not remove His blessing and love because we are grown and old. Not only for their children, but also for their great-grandchildren and many more to come.

Faith and Prayer

Our parents taught us to pray with faith, knowing nothing is impossible with God. Prayer with faith can change any situation. There is a family friend who, as a young man, mother would always pray with him. She would encourage him to live his life as service unto God. As this young man got older, he developed some medical problems. As he made his three score years in life, his condition continued to deteriorate. On one of our visits, surprisingly, he told us about our mother's encouraging words and prayers with him.

The following year he became critically ill. So, we paid him a family visit. I reminded him of mother's prayer as she prayed with him and faith in God. I knew this would be our last visit. I was prepared of the call about him leaving us at any time. He is a well-known man in his community. If God can use anyone, He can use him. One night, upon returning home a few days later, I decided to say a special prayer for his recovery. I prayed that God would restore him for his purpose and that people would know nothing is impossible with God. He can use anyone for His service. Occasionally I would call to check on his condition and I was told he was improving.

After a few months had past, we decided to pay him a visit. I called the house to see what time was best to visit only to be told he was not there. My heart sank. I asked what happened to him. With urgency, I was told he was okay and out with family. My response was "what? I have to see it to believe it. Please call me when he's home."

We went and visited him on his return home. He was up eating and walking with a walker. He gave us his testimony. He prayed and asked God to raise him up for His service and let His will be done. He told us how he settled his debt with a man. They both was indebted to each other. After paying each other, the man was still owing him. He told the man to put the balance in the offering plate when he goes to church. He stated his reason for doing so. He wanted nothing to worry about when God is ready to take him home. He was confident God heard his prayer and relieved his suffering; giving him more time. He reflected on the times mother prayed with him. Again, God does hear and answer prayer. I have learnt some very important lessons in regard to the result of answered prayers.

Whenever you pray, have faith your prayers will be answered. You have to be willing to do your part. Prayers answered in abundance is not meant for you alone. You need to bless others abundantly and watch your blessings flow. Growing up, it was a few of us children at home. However, whatever blessing, great or small, comes mother's way, she was always sharing with the neighbors. She would always say, "when God blesses you, bless someone else. Care not how small it may be. Put a smile on someone's face, feed someone, or a family. Give the needy some help. Hardship can hit anyone at any time. Always be caring and giving. I live by these rules and it's fulfilling."

One year while visiting home on vacation, I attended a church function there and ran into a few of my classmates. We were so excited and happy to see each other as we are now all grown mothers, grandmothers, fathers and grandfathers. We were all catching up on our career paths, children and their achievement and we continued down memory lane. While there, I was reminded of mother feeding and praying with them as kids either at Bible school or on the farm during the summer holidays. She would encourage them to do their best in school, always pray asking God to bless and provide for their needs. I think we were all blessed and giving back to the community that raised us to be the men and women we are today. Prayers answered and his great blessings indeed.

God's Favor

When you are taught to pray for God's direction and guidance on your life, it's hard for you to forget such teaching as you get older and experience the need for God's interventions. If you live your life as service unto God, He will put His blessing and favor on your life. At times, when you can't see your way through, if you pray with faith, God will show you His favor in His time and own way. We must always remember God does not work on our time but wait patiently for His response to our prayer.

At times it may seem as if God do not hear your prayers, but he does again and again. His time is not your time. He will bestow His blessing and favor as He sees best for our needs. We need to remember when He blesses us, we are to bless someone else generously.

Life is like a road. It has rough areas and smooth areas. It has holes and patches. Life's path can be curved, straight and also has twist and turns. It has narrow and wide paths on mountains and in valleys. At times, it's dry or wet. However, with God's blessing, grace and mercy, He will help us navigate our way through life. We should strive to leave good memories on this path we call life.

In life, one should be attentive, caring, devoted, empathetic, grateful, happy, honest, kind, loving, patient, thoughtful and tolerant. These are spices for a good life which ca be beautiful. We enter this world by the same process called birth. We leave this world by the same process called death. In between these processes is called life. We should enjoy life while living in this beautiful creation called earth. Take some time and travel to different places in this world and see the beauty of God's creation. Enjoy the beauty of the mountains, the smell of the vast ocean and the beautiful green pastures and valleys. Get to know and respect different culture, places and people.

God is still performing miracles today.

You may be facing your Rea Sea or Lion Den. I want you to know that God can deliver you. Like He delivered the children of Israel at the Red Sea and Daniel in the Lion's Den.

Talk to God. He will hear you in whatever situation you are in. Be honest when talking to God. Especially when asking for forgiveness. Remember He created you with the ability to speak and think. Therefore, He will know if you are honest before you start speaking.

Chapter Two

My Prayer Answered and My Change Came

As a child my dream was to become a doctor and to travel the world. Financially my parents were unable to support my dream, but their prayers were good enough. My prayer was answered in 1977 when I was accepted at the Kingston School of Nursing in the 3 year program. I successfully completed the course and graduated in 1980. My parents were very happy for my achievement. Their words to me were, "you are now at the beginning of life and at the end of life. We will continue to pray for you. You will need to pray for guidance to care for the sick."

My change came in 1984 when I migrated to the United States, New York. I met people of many different culture, nationality and Religion. I was blessed to be of service caring for people from different parts of the world. Meeting all these different nationalities inspired me more to see the world. I am blessed to see many of Caribbean Island and some places in Africa and in Europe.

There is an observation that is very important to me. We are all God's children needing love and care. I'm very happy answering God's call to be of service to His children. Continue to pray for God's guidance on your life daily. I hope I have brightened your day and you are willing to give GOD a try. Remember, after darkness comes the light.

Thank you to my family and friends who believed in me and encouraged me. May God continue to bless you all, love always.

The Magical Power of My Praying Parents

www.ingramcontent.com/pod-product-compliance
Lightning Source LLC
Chambersburg PA
CBHW071917160426
42813CB00098B/533